The Bear Suit

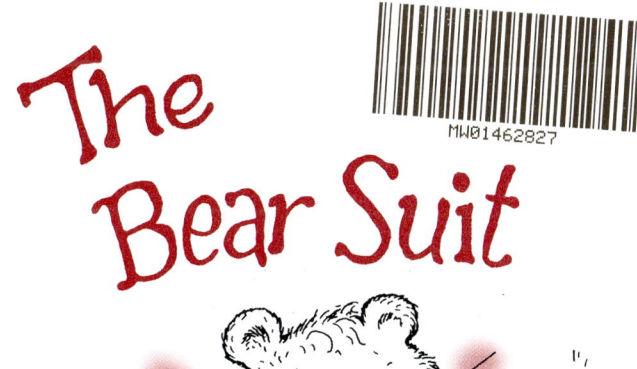

By Cass Hollander
Illustrations by Sheila Lucas

Harcourt Brace & Company
Orlando Atlanta Austin Boston San Francisco Chicago Dallas New York Toronto London

Bart Charles and Clair Clark were invited to a costume party at Margo Park's house. "I'm wearing a shark suit," said Bart. "What will you wear, Clair?"

"I'm wearing a hairy bear suit," said Clair. "Margo's house isn't far from mine. Let's meet in my yard. We'll go to the party as a pair."

"A shark and a hairy bear! We'll scare everyone!" cried Bart.

"We'll be a charming, scary pair!" said Clair.

Bart laughed. "Clair, don't be scared or alarmed when you see a shark in your yard!"

Bart went home to prepare for the party. It was starting to get dark, so Mrs. Charles drove Bart the Shark to Clair's yard.

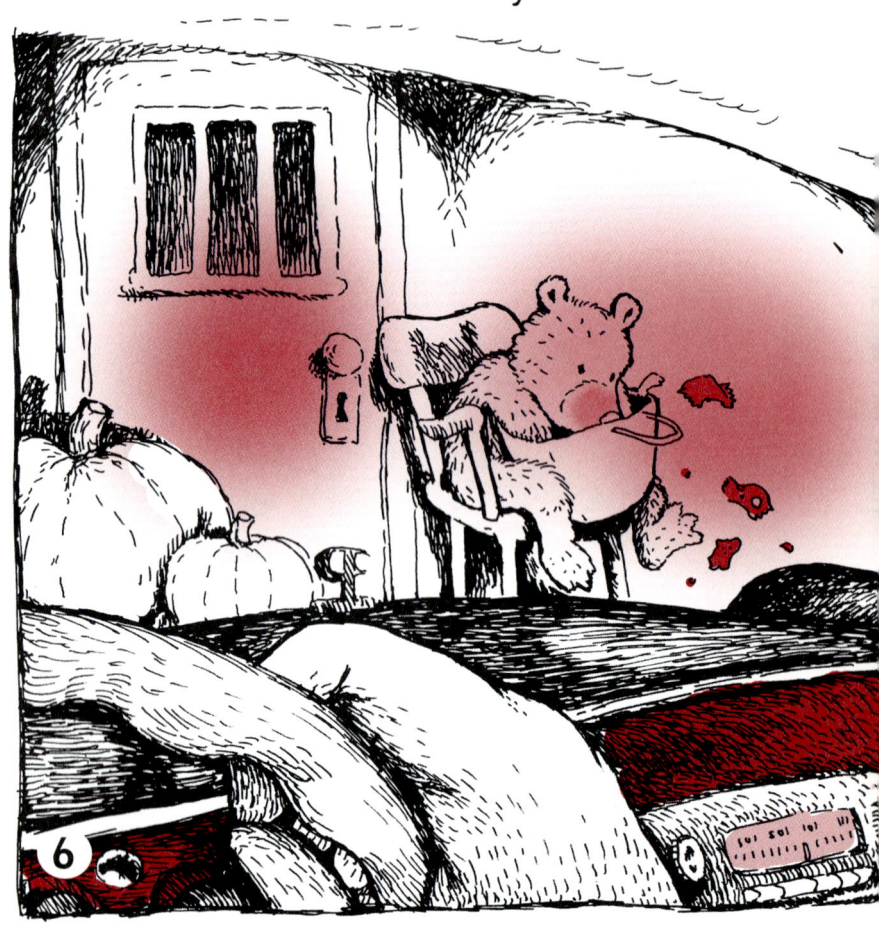

A hairy bear was sitting in a chair on Clair's porch.

"There's Clair!" said Bart. "She's wearing her hairy bear suit. Isn't it neat?"

"Bears don't sit in chairs!" Bart said as he got out of the car. "Come on, Clair! Start acting like a bear!"

Bart laughed. "Clair," Bart said, "you really are a scary, hairy bear." The scary, hairy, bear just sat and stared.

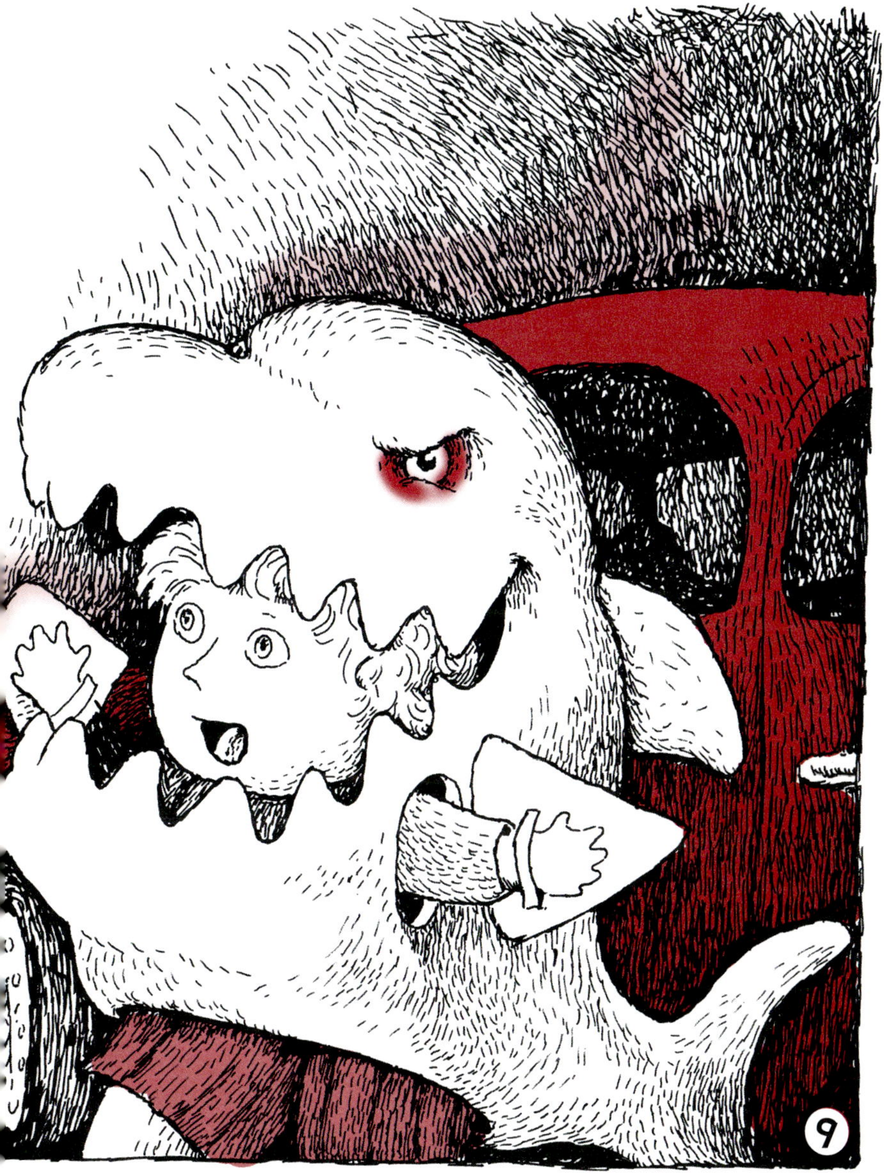

Bart stared at the hairy bear. "I'm glad it's you, Clair," said Bart. "I wouldn't care to share the yard with a real hairy bear."

The hairy bear in the chair just looked at Bart. "Is your to suit made of yarn?" Bart asked. "It looks like real bear hair! And your claws look sharp!"

The hairy bear stared and snarled at Bart. Bart stared harder at the hairy bear. Bart marched up the stairs. "You look like a scary bear, Clair!"

The hairy bear in the chair bared its teeth. "Let's start for the party, Clair," said Bart. "Will anyone guess who the scary bear and scary shark are? What a nightmare pair!"

Clair's dog Barney barked. The hairy bear charged down the stairs.

"Smart!" said Bart. "Barney thinks you're a bear, Clair! You even run like a bear! But no fair running. It's hard to run in this shark suit."

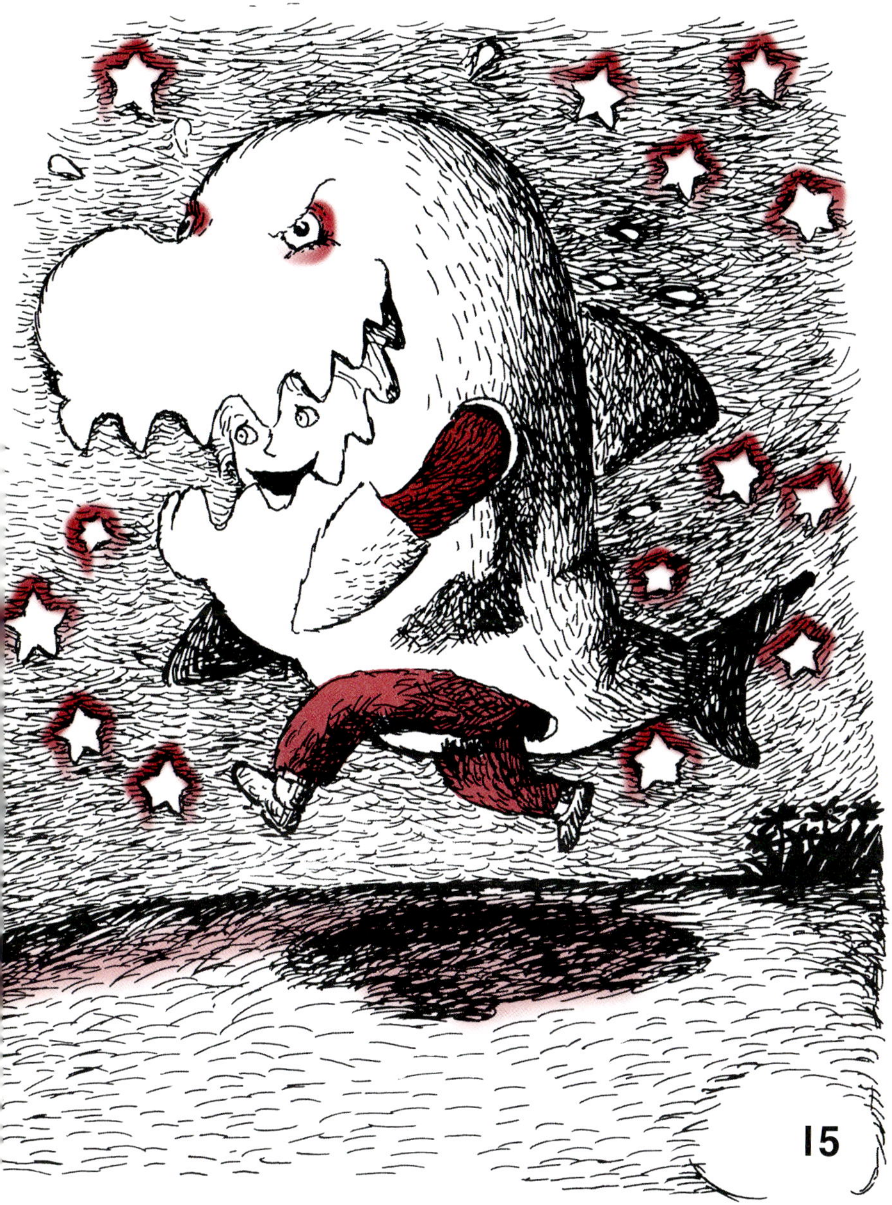

Just then another hairy bear darted down the stairs. This hairy bear didn't glare or snarl. "Bart, wait!" said this hairy bear. "How dare you start for Margo's party without me!"